THE MYSTERIOUS MAN

LYUBOMIR LEVCHEV

The Mysterious Man

Translated by

Vladimir Phillipov

OHIO UNIVERSITY PRESS
Chicago   Athens, Ohio   London
International Poetry Series
Volume IV

FOREWORD

This is the fourth book in the International Poetry Forum's
Byblos Series. The first was Marco Antonio Montes de
Oca's *The Heart of the Flute* translated by Laura Villaseñor
with an introduction by Octavio Paz. The second was
Artur Lundkvist's *Agadir* translated and with an introduc-
tion by William Jay Smith and Leif Sjöberg. Yannis Ritsos'
Subterranean Horses in a translation by Minas Savvas
and with an introduction by Vassilis Vassilikos was the
third selection. The present volume is in the same tradition
of providing the best translations of some of the most
significant poets in the world for an audience that would
not otherwise be able to read them in their own languages.

Samuel Hazo
Director

CONTENTS

THE LAND OF MURDERED POETS

Between the Arctic circle
and the Tropic of Cancer
(between passion
and reason),
far away
from the sky
there blooms a land
—beautiful
and rich—
the land of murdered poets . . .

Yet verses surge;
they press on darkly
and tear me to pieces.
And there,
following tradition,
the reaper swings
his scythe
of sunshine.
"You are still alive!"—
The eagle is insulted.
The wolf is searching
with its eyes
for wounds.

Earth for me!
Earth deep in me!
The earth is shrieking
in my sleepless nights.
The turbulent river of my blood
is washing away
the banks of my heart.
And I learn
how to write poetry
in the land of murdered poets.

POSITIONS

We are not schoolmates;
neither have we struck a friendship
over a glass of brandy.
We have taken positions
in the same trench
where two worlds are warring.
The world of the gods in twilight
counter-attacks every day.
The hours flow quickly
like blood.
It is so good
you are next to me!
I thank you
without a word,
without a look.
We don't even know
each other's name.
That is why
under the whistling bullets
we are brothers.

But when this battle ends,
we shall search
each other's eyes!
And probably we shall be amazed to find,
that they are absolutely different.
You'll say:
"I am fond of silence."
I'll say:
"I am fond of jazz."
We'll smile at our names.
And then: "Good-bye!"
It won't be late,
nor early,
for the nameless winds,
and nameless birds . . .
Only those who die
will keep their positions.

POETRY READINGS

Poetry readings,
poetry readings! . . .
From small student clubs
to halls for festive proceedings,
against windmills,
against ghosts,
and the hosts
of weekdays,
and with no armour . . .
the poet follows his poetry on and on
the way Sancho Panza follows his Don!

Well, of course,
everyone receives bouquets
on certain days.
But there are small distant towns!
A railway station.
Dogs barking.
Heaps of sugar beets and empty crates . . .
And again
we slip down slowly
from the evening train.
Beneath the signal-bell
waiting for us
is that nervous youth,
that eternal
          unknown
                    brother of ours,
who summons us like spirits into his world.
Always "on behalf of all from the construction-site"
who "admire those who poetry write . . ."

All right.
We set off on patrol silently.
The shortcut looks like a cornfield.
But against the sky-line
          like heroin
                    excitedly shine
the bright
electrical flowers of the construction-site.
And in dining room No. 2
amid the smell of stew

we speak to you,
Twentieth Century!
"You are stained with the blood
of dreams
and deceptions!
You need poets,
mad but divine!
We will sweep your skies
free of every mine! . . ."

Oh, we promise wonderful miracles.
But the handful of fitters
who've come to hear us
                    whisper.
They are not impressed—
they go out for a smoke.
Their eyes are blue with pure perplexity:
"What is this poet
trying to tell us! . . ."
Poets can survive everything—
they can starve
and sing,
be unemployed or expelled . . .

But God,
        can they do without applause?
Put on a grin!
Say it doesn't matter.
But your soul is empty
completely.
                    Defeat!
                    Defeat!
And so,
in the dining cars
we've often washed our wounds with liquor,
and someone of us would sadly snicker:
"Well, Zhenya Evtushenko
        recites his poetry
                    in stadiums!"
That,
     old mate,
                is Russian—
they listen to you
even if you aren't great . . .
Even if they don't understand a word.

It's absurd,
but in some place like New York
they will applaud . . .''

O God !
Verses are not for stadiums!
Verses are read in sacred hours.
Like love letters.
Like subversive leaflets.
Which require no affectation,
                    but dedication . . .

The return train
reaches its destination,
and the poets disperse
to their old lodgings,
and to new battle fields . . .
I too was going home,
late at night,
passing the stadium . . .

when suddenly I noticed
that the fence was ripped.
A smile dawned on me.
And I crept in like a memory from the past,
through the deserted stands,
into the vast
arena.

An abandoned bottle
rang down the steps
like an absurd bell
in the absurd amphitheater.
And then . . .
This romantic adventure
            got hold of me.
Three million stars
were sitting on the benches
watching me.
And I began to recite
with a surprising voice.
My most sincere passion
echoed selfless in the night.
I think I spoke about the stars.
How man rises like a sun.

And how difficult it is to shine,
with his own light
                    at that,
and turn into ashes
over new foundations
and honest lines . . .

If there was a watchman around,
he must have thought I was mad.
But you see,
I couldn't care less about it.
So real was this recital of mine,
that you can envy me!

TRUMPETER

I love the twilight.
Like a legendary trumpeter,
stained by blood
but eternal,
it sounds the retreat.

I cannot hear it . . .
But the colors hear it,
the constellations hear it
and rise.

This is the time
to lie on the warm earth,
caressed by the caring grass,
to drink star juice
in small gulps,
to think in small gulps:

"Why do our eyes
see so far?
Now I cannot hear
the evening train
dashing away in the valley
with my youth on it . . .
Now I am not aware
of the white butterfly
caught in my hair . . .
But I can see the cosmos?
Why?
That makes no sense.
Why have I been programed
to see the endless space?
Why have we been placed
face to face
with the unattainable?"

Stars!
Aren't you the nails of the universe?
What has been fastened with you?
I'll never know . . .

However,
your victorious armies
pass through my eyes
as through a triumphal arch,
and greet mother-infinity . . .

My weariness
wears away.
A new thirst
thrusts up in me.

CONFESSION AND GREETINGS TO THE FIRE

The interrogators
are the whips of my imperfections,
I collapse . . .
and confess.

I confess
that poetry
is a criminal attempt
to translate
the pulsations of the universe
into the ordinary language of our hearts.

I confess
that poetry
is wicked witchcraft
which gives divinities
the image of man,
and brands man with the sign of the divine.

I confess
that I've always known
that one dies at the stake
for practicing witchcraft.

And yet,
I greet
our life-giving and destructive
poetic fire!

I kiss your ashes,
brothers and sisters of mine,
who have perished at the stake!
I give myself to you,
our fiery red,
fighting love!

DAMN YOU, COLUMBUS!

Don Cristobal Colon,
or Columbus,
or whatever you call yourself,
you are
a naive,
and stupid
wretch . . .
There's no mercy for you!

Why didn't you listen
to the admiral on the solid land
who whispered in your ear:
"Take care, my friend,
take care! . . .
You drink of the storms
and the endless space,
but don't forget
that it's important for me
with whom I drink my tea! . . ."

O Lord!
don't you see that the noblemen of Spain
are bored?
Columbus,
the rumor has it
that you are a scoundrel,
that you travel to the West
not to increase our treasure
but for your own pleasure . . .
that the route you've discovered
does not go to India,
but God only knows where . . .

And also—
that instead of praying to God
you drink a lot,
that you're a lecher . . .
Damn you, Columbus!
Damn you!

You know
what is in store for you.

Your continent will bear the name
of someone else,
and for you—
the whip, disdain,
syphilis, and ruin too! . . .

Don Cristobal Colon,
why aren't you miserable?

Why aren't you crawling in fear?
Why are you lying
unperturbed
on the pier
together with the leprous sailors?

You are looking at something.
Is it a cloud,
or a ghost,
or a host of stellar star-fish? . . .
You're an abominable man!
A monster!
Again you see something
which we cannot see . . .
Damn you!

A SONG TO GARCÍA LORCA

*"When I die . . .
bury me with a guitar . . ."*

—GARCÍA LORCA

Where is that gory Granada?
Where is your grave?
Whom should I ask?
The fiery horses
that snort
and scratch the earth
with restless hoofs,
or the bearded eagles
of rugged Nevada? . . .

Granada
is too far . . .
Are the skies there
blue or gray?
What are the myrtles
which grow
in Granada?
I do not know.
But I do know
that you died
for Granada,
that the blood-stained shirts
of brothers of mine
have rotted
in the Spanish earth,
where the seguidilla's heard . . .
Granada
is far away,
but you are not.

I want to find your grave
not to cry and grieve,
but to sing
a song
and pick the waiting strings
of my guitar.
I want to whet
on the stone of your grave
a Castilian knife
of the strongest metal
for the coming battle.

THE EVENING BOYS

When there is
a little sadness,
a little darkness,
and a little of
"What shall we do,"
then
the evening boys
spring out
of the indifferent pavements,
bare-chested.
They are wicked
and content.
They have become
what they cannot be.
Tired values surrender to them
inversed.
Lips out of reach
whisper:
"Darling! . . ."
The forbidden hour:
"Forget! . . ."

Don't stop.
Don't turn around.
. . . They are striding
and spitting
along the main street.

We look at them
with frightened contempt.
We are not "roughs"
and that is enough . . .

But deep down in us
there is also
a little sadness,
and a little darkness.

But we . . . we know
what we live for.
We are all right
because we are upright.

Shadowy people jostle
under our high slogans.

Promenades!
Parades of meaningless instincts,
of unfulfilled dreams,
parades of evening boys.

For many evenings.
For many years.
Along the cruelly familiar pavement
—from the dark city park
to the monument
of the men
who have been hanged . . .

MEN EQUAL TO HEAVEN

I saw two street-cleaners
washing the street at night.
A warning thunder
traversed the sky,
as if up there
someone else was rolling
a similar hose-drum
along a similarly cobbled street.
Soon afterwards
it began to rain.
The lights of the town started running
like the make-up of a crying woman.
A woman ran across the garden.
A window pane broke with a crash . . .
But the two street-cleaners
and the serpent
went on unperturbed.
This was their job!
                They had to do it!
Even though heaven had decided
to wash together with them.
This was a job!
                They had to do it!
It was raining.
The cleaners were washing.
The heavens flared up—
              now red,
                now orange.
Almost rhythmically
like traffic lights.
So that the cleaners flared too—
now red,
       now orange,
almost rhythmically . . .
I had not seen men more heavenly
than those two elderly men
who continued washing the street
together with heaven . . .

Yes,
(though rarely)
man is equal to heaven!

MY MEMORY OF A HISTORY TEXTBOOK

The shots have become too many!

Will the Loch Ness monster rise again?
Will the crusading epidemic spread?
Will the teutonic drum beat roll?
        "O eternal ideals! . . ."
        "Ancient frontiers! . . ."
        "Destiny and fate! . . ."

I am well aware of these shelters
made of words.
Cartridge shells of brass,
toys for orphans
still jingling in the torn pocket
of my memory . . .

"Margery. Three. Over.
Margery. Three. Over."
I still hear
death communicating something
to someone.

Ours was a very small town.
A single siren
was enough to sound the alarm
in everyone.
And every one of us
came out on the balconies—
inquisitive,
ready to offer ourselves in sacrifice.
But the terrifying flying fortresses
flew over us
with their four-engined grumble:
"Worthless midgets!
We cannot even see you!
All of you, taken together,
are not worth the price
of one single bomb . . ."

And yet our little town
was proud,
and had an air-raid shelter of its own.

An air-raid shelter!
As if the earth
had opened its mouth
to cry out something.
What?
One day I skipped school
and hid in the air-raid shelter.
It smelled of mud and roots.
The palate over me kept dripping.
But I was eternal
and ancient! . . .
I took out my fearless history book.
The pages turned into torches.
And the lesson about the golden age of Pericles
lit up this throat of the void.
Then Rome and Nero were burnt.
Hundred-year wars.
And Bastilles.
And sacred territories.
Invincible armies . . .

I reached the end—
the end of the shelter.
It boomed like a flying fortress,
and like a fire-bomb exploded.
I bolted back to the field,
the dew,
and the blue air . . .

And the sinister laughter of the teacher,
the consumptive Herr Odotus:
"Historia est magistra vitae!"
Funny memories,
aren't they?

And so—
beware of your shelters!
The most terrible thing
man has contrived
are shelters!
No matter what we call them—
anti-gas,
or anti-A-bomb . . .
No matter what they are made of—

concrete,
or fanfares,
or rhymes,
or stupidity . . .

THE GOOD SAMARITAN

I walk along an ancient country road,
cut by caterpillar chains.
In the cathedral of the empty afternoon
silence gives me the sacrament
and I become good,
almost as good
as the good Samaritan.

I walk along an ancient country road,
admiring the sunflowers,
admiring their loyalty,
how all of them,
but all
are turned towards the sun!
And how they look at it! . . .
But see,
there is among them one,
a single one,
which has turned its back to the sun.
It immediately becomes
my sunflower.

I run towards it.
Prickly leaves lick my cheeks.
I stumble over lumps of earth and stubble.
I embrace my sunflower
and lovingly try
to show it
what the right direction is.
Without a word it turns again
towards the heretic side.
The sunflower is mad,
fanatic.
Having looked at the sun too long,
it looks like the sun.
I try to discover
what it is staring at.
There is just the sky
and nothing else.
Dark blue ridges,
the smoke of a train,

a slow,
        distant
             ghost . . .

My confused friend,
tell me something
about your imaginary sun!
Is it square,
or black?
Or an obscure creature?
A lonely proof?
A soldier's wound? . . .

My sunflower keeps
scornful silence.

Brown ants creep up
along the stems of all sunflowers
and along mine too.
The trace
of a jet plane
curves overhead
like a whip.
I walk along an ancient country road.

THE SHOT

They left me in a tree,
on a balcony among the branches
which is called the stalking place . . .
Then the sleigh went away.
The children's bells melted away.
I was all alone.

I was all alone.
In the last wood of my world.
In the last real wood.
A wood with beasts
and brown elves,
and a silence
resinous
and cold . . .

I felt
I was freezing in the silence.
I opened my gun and looked through the barrel.
I saw through it—
the volcano Fujiyama—
a peaceful sacred mountain . . .
Or perhaps what I saw
was death
        lying in wait.
And since I know
that death does not wait long,
I quickly filled my end of the barrel
with two beautiful cartridges for deer.
And then I heard the deer approach.—
Its antlers crackled in the scrub
like a blazing fire.
At the edge of the glade
the deer looked around
and bent its head
as if to kiss the earth.
In fact it was looking for the salt . . .

I took aim
and held my breath.
Then the red whip
cracked with its incredible strength.

The deer jumped,
straight towards the sky
like a fountain
when children play with the tap,
and crumbled into the snow.
And then the mysterious duel started.
An agony which looked like love gone wild.
In love with nothingness.
O, Death!

I climbed down the tree,
sent the second bullet into the head,
not to spoil the skin.
I pulled out the still steaming cartridge-cases . . .
But dropped them into the blood.
Because that very moment
the soul of the deer
fluttered over me.
Or did the wood moan?
The last wood of my world.
And the trampled wind.

JOURNEYING TOWARDS THE SETTING SUN

I see
the lonely children of J. Alfred Prufrock
lying about the corridors and steps
of railway stations.
Eyes staring at the nothing
like temples plundered by barbarians.
Tattooed chests
and bared thighs.
And the bared tracks of love
like the tracks of a snail.
The train too, which will never arrive,
and will never depart
for them . . .
The faces are so familiar!
The long hair,
the pointed beard . . .!
Richard the Lion Hearted
is sleeping over there
by the spittoon.
Under the time table
Bloody Mary
is searching for a vein
for her heroin.
Thomas Becket
is cleaning his dirty nails
with the treacherous cross
of Canterbury . . .
O Lord!
has history vomited
after guzzling on an empty stomach?
It can't continue that way any longer!
It can't continue!
It can't!

THE HAIDUCK* HERB

It does not have to declare
its loyalty to our native land.
It blossoms like a wintry legend
and does not care
how its credit fares.
Flaming wounds it heals,
and it inflames love.
It's called
the Haiduck herb . . .

That's what it is to me . . .

But to the people?
To the atom-anxious world?
What is it to them?
A half-proved item
in the tiresome herbarium—
Betonica Bulgarica—
a root which refuses to grow
in the Pyrenees,
the Andes,

or the Himalayas,
but only in the shady Balkans . . .

. . . And only in my heart . . .

Betonica Bulgarica—
the Haiduck herb.
The old quacks
still go out in the witching hour
in search for it.
They drawl
and snoop
and scratch.
They pull it out of the earth
and out of my heart.
Then they boil it in dirty pots,
mumble incantations over it
and sell it on the sly

---

*Haiduck—a revolutionary fighter for liberty in Bulgaria during the
period of Ottoman domination.

as a charm against the thirst for traveling,
as a medicine against outlandish diseases . . .

To hell with all old quacks! . . .

I am "afflicted" with an idea,
international in its origin!
I do not know the number of roads ahead of me.
I do not know under what sky
I'll fight my final battle . . .

If a bullet strikes down my brother,
the lemon yellow one,
or the white one,
or the one with the complexion of despair,
I will appear
to breathe my breath into him
and tell him
"I am called the Haiduck herb;
my name is Betonica Bulgarica."
I'll kiss his wound
and it will heal
as in the fairy-tales.
Then we will run together
                    round the red earth
and sing!
Liberty!
Liberty!
Liberty!

THE DAY MOON

The world is made
of earth, skies and "whys."
I too,
like all,
am trying
to make things clear,
to turn form into formula,
and knowledge into usefulness . . .
But why,
when reading the latest news in the train,
or later on,
when listening
to the boss's pompous voice,
why do I keep an eye
on the sky?
Why do I feel your presence,
day moon,
unnoticeable,
like the scar of vaccination?
Why?
. . . In the cafeteria,
or when finishing an urgent article,
why can't I stop thinking of you?
You distract me,
day moon,—
a transparent white ghost,—
a secret . . .
Why are you there on such a sunny afternoon?
Have you stayed behind?
Or are you premature?
This might be all the same to you . . .
But not to me!
I am transient.
Short-lived like my verse.
I try to make things clear . . .
You are a piece of bridal veil,
thrown into the blue!
Are you
          a memory of nights gone-by
or a presentiment of things
which lie in the future,
in darkness?

SALT

There is one final urge,
a childish desire
which sends the old people
off to the sea.

Are they in search of something to come?
Or do they want to see what they've lost?

The sea roars like blood pressure.
With funny parasols
and funny hats
brought from the deep inland,
the old ones
hurry
hurry
to hear the twin of heaven . . .

But there . . .
they draw away
carefully avoiding the beach,
carefully avoiding the casino,
they make their way
through the vineyards
towards the old salt-pans.
Suddenly the grass around gets red.
They wade into a hot and shallow mirror.
But this is the sea,
        this is the sea,
                the sea.
A sense of the infinite invades their fluttering souls.
Someone starts a song a thousand years old.
The pitiless sun turns round its halo,
The water in the square evaporates.
And all that's left of the old people
are cones and salt.

THE MYSTERIOUS MAN

Man is a mystery!

There—
an elderly mystery
is walking in the thin sun.
She is smiling.
She is saying to herself:
"I'll unriddle myself
tomorrow!"

Two other mysteries
are waiting in a line
at the green-grocer's.
They are gossiping secretly:
"I must say to you
that nothing remains secret
under the sun!
. . . It is all true!"

At this moment
the small bells of the church
start jingling
like coins
in the bluish pocket of the sky.
Another pair of secrets
—naive and transparent . . .

O Lord!
I don't think
I shall ever get bored!

THE POLAR CIRCLE

An endless Scandinavian night—
a rehearsal of death . . .
But I stay awake.
Like dog's eyes
the stars
disappear
and then,
they fix on me again.
White doubt
filters in,
and I notice
I am not that young anymore . . .
What good is this movement of mine?
Is this world beyond redemption?
Do not the scientists,
paid by the richest trusts,
prove today
that the cosmos is expanding,
galaxies are drawing away,
space is emptying,
everything is growing cold,
alienated,
like the past
from the future . . .
And I . . .
I try to bring together!
                 To unite!

Ridiculous,
and doomed to failure . . .!
I detest all pessimistic prophets!

If God wills,
let Him sell the space
above his domains
to contractors!

Now I prefer
to listen to nature
in the endless Scandinavian night . . .

It is cold.
I hear the whining
of a universal whirlwind.
Like a wild dog
the shivering cosmos
huddles round my heart in search of warmth,
warmth from a human heart.

Just for a minute
of a twentieth century,
of an eternity . . .!

VITAE

Lyubomir Levchev was born in Troyan, Bulgaria, on April 27, 1935. After being graduated from Sofia University with concentrations in philosophy and history, he worked on the staff of the newspaper *Narodna Mladezh* and subsequently with Radio Sofia. He then became editor of the weekly *Literatouren Front.* After his appointment as Deputy Chairman of the National Council of the Father-land Front, he became First Deputy President of the Art and Culture Committee. He is now President of the Union of Bulgarian Writers. A prolific author, Levchev has had his books translated into many languages and has traveled extensively.

Vladimir Phillipov is a member of the English Department of Sofia University. He has taught in the United States and made numerous translations of the work of Bulgarian writers.

Originally published as Volume IV of the Byblos Editions, International Poetry Forum, in a limited edition of two hundred copies. The text is set in Monotype Univers.